D1238329
- 2014

The TACO REVOLUTION

10 9 8 7 6 5 4 3 2 1

Library of Congress Cataloging-in-Publication Data

Schultz, Brandon, 1984-
The taco revolution : over 100 traditional and innovative recipes to master America's new favorite food

ISBN 978-1-62873-623-6 (hardback)

1. Tacos. 2. Salsas. 3. Mexican American cooking. I. Title.
TX836.S38 2014
641.84—dc23

2013039265

Printed in China

Over 100 Traditional and Innovative Recipes
to Master America's New Favorite Food

By Brandon Schultz

SKYHORSE PUBLISHING

To Joanne and Joann, for endless inspiration in cuisine and hospitality, and infectious enthusiasm for food.

TABLE OF CONTENTS

INTRODUCTION

If you still think *ground beef, lettuce, tomato, cheese, and salsa* when you hear "taco," you are missing out on a world of flavorful opportunities that could change the way you think about every meal of the day! A taco is simply a meal in a tortilla and, while traditional tacos typically involve slow-cooked meats, you can put just about anything in a tortilla with delicious results. Fruit? Macaroni and cheese? Chinese food? YES! Breakfast? Lunch? Dinner? YES!

If you are merely curious, the recipes that follow could keep you busy with new tacos for a year as you mix and match the various tortilla shells, stuffings, seasonings, and sauces. If you are adventurous, the recipes could inspire you for a lifetime as you branch out into your own creations with the techniques learned here. Be creative and remember a few simple guidelines: nothing too runny or wet, nothing too hard or crunchy (except in very small doses), smaller ingredients usually work better, and a large piece of lettuce goes further than shredded lettuce when it comes to keeping a tortilla dry or containing ingredients if a tortilla breaks!

Only recently has the taco become a phenomenon, with taco food trucks and restaurants popping up everywhere, but tacos have been around for thousands of years, and for good reasons: They are simple, filling, and delicious! Here is everything you need to master traditional tacos, try modern takes, and invent your own. All recipes that include specific tortillas, sauces, or salsas are simply my suggestions based on what I found to go best with the stuffings, but you can and *should* substitute to your own taste. And if you are preparing tacos for several people, provide as many options as you can; every taco can be personally tailored to heat profiles, allergy considerations, and topping preferences without any added work for the chef! Tacos are a win for everyone, all the time, so get started!

EQUIPMENT

At the bare minimum, you do not *need* anything special to create great tacos, but there are a couple of tools that can make your life a lot easier, especially if you plan to make tacos often.

CAST-IRON PAN

A cast-iron pan is going to be the most reliable tool for heating anything evenly, and this is an enormous benefit when making a tortilla, which is thin and cooks very quickly. You can make tortillas without one, but if you have been considering investing in cast iron already, then consider this your justification for finally doing it. One cast-iron pan is not a huge expense, and it will make your culinary life easier far beyond tacos!

TORTILLA PRESS

If you are going to make your own tortillas, and I absolutely suggest you do, a tortilla press is a cheap investment (about $20) that will yield perfect tortillas with minimal struggle every time! If you have a great eye for circles and refuse to have one more kitchen gadget in your life, you can use a rolling pin, but this method will be a bit more difficult, considerably messier, and will rarely give you a nice, round result. If you do not care, skip it! I love mine. (It can also be very helpful for baking!)

DUTCH OVEN

I use a Dutch oven when preparing meats for most of the recipes in *The Taco Revolution* because it ensures a juicier result. Dry meat will kill a taco. If you do not have one, and do not want one, a pot with a tight lid will work well in most cases.

GRIDDLE

A griddle is great for recipes like the Philly Cheeseteak Taco where a good amount of thin meat should be cooked quickly while possibly being chopped and shredded at the same time. This can be achieved in a flat-bottomed pan, just in smaller batches.

FOOD PROCESSOR

Especially for salsa and sauce recipes, a food processor can make your taco life much easier, but this is not essential. A traditional blender (or immersion blender) will do the job, but with a little more time and probably less perfect results.

ICE CREAM MAKER, SMOKER & JULIENNE PEELER

Each of these is featured in exactly one recipe in *The Taco Revolution*. If you are determined to try every single recipe (and I hope you are!), then you need these. If not, skip them, but be warned: The three recipes you are forfeiting are delicious, and regrets can keep you up at night. . . .

BEEF

Cheeseburger Taco
Cheesy Lettuce Wrap Taco
Classic American Taco
Greek Taco
Navajo Taco
Philly Cheesesteak Taco
Reuben Taco
Santa Fe Taco Salad
Traditional Taco Salad

Cheeseburger Taco

Have a craving for a burger outside of grilling season? Looking for something fun for kids or a party? The cheeseburger taco is even easier than a traditional burger, with fewer ingredients and more flavor!

Makes 6 tacos.
1 pound ground beef
1 cup cheddar cheese, shredded
1½ cups torn lettuce (large pieces)
1 plum tomato, diced
¼ cup red onion, thinly sliced
½ cup relish
Cheddar cheese, shredded, for topping
Tortillas

Directions:

1. Brown ground beef in a large pan over medium-high heat, about 8-10 minutes. Add cheddar cheese and cook 1 more minute, mixing constantly, until fully melted.
2. Top a tortilla with lettuce, tomato, and red onion. Add cheesy ground beef and top with relish and a sprinkling of shredded cheddar cheese.

Cheesy Lettuce Wrap Taco

Traditional tacos are naturally gluten-free, but if you only have flour tortillas on hand and still need a gluten-free alternative, lettuce wraps are the perfect solution. They work particularly well with this recipe but can be applied to any taco that is not overly wet or crunchy.

Makes 4-6 tacos.
1 pound ground beef
1 cup cheddar cheese, shredded
4-6 large leaves iceberg lettuce, whole
1 plum tomato, diced
¼ cup red onion, thinly sliced
Cheddar cheese, shredded, for topping
½ cup sour cream, for topping

Directions:

1. Brown ground beef in a large pan over medium-high heat, about 8-10 minutes. Add cheddar cheese and cook 1 more minute, mixing constantly, until fully melted.
2. Top a lettuce leaf with cheesy beef, tomato, and red onion. Sprinkle cheddar cheese and top with sour cream. Serve open, and wrap/roll loosely to eat.

Classic American Taco

This is probably what you envision when you hear the word "taco," and it is the only taco in this book specifically recommended for the baked shell. Of course, you can use any shell you like, any time, but something about this taco begs for the crunch that only comes with a baked shell!

Makes 8-10 tacos.
½ pound ground beef
1½ Tablespoons Classic Taco Seasoning (page 170)
½ cup water
1 cup sour cream
2 cups iceberg lettuce, shredded
2 plum tomatoes, diced
Baked Tortillas (page 138)
Mild Salsa (page 194), to be served on the side

DIRECTIONS:
1. Brown ground beef in a large pan over medium-high heat, about 8-10 minutes. Drain excess grease, add Classic Taco Seasoning and ½ cup water, and simmer until water is mostly evaporated, about 6-8 minutes.
2. Layer 1 teaspoon of sour cream on the bottom of a tortilla (sour cream on the bottom helps hold ingredients together when the shell begins to crack!). Top with lettuce, tomato, and beef.
3. Serve with Mild Salsa (or Hot Salsa, if preferred!) on the side.

Note: Many people enjoy taco sauce, especially if using soft tortillas. See Mild Taco Sauce (page 204) and Hot Taco Sauce (page 204) for options!

Greek Taco

For a more adult flavor profile in a beef taco, try this Greek-inspired recipe.

Makes 4-6 tacos.
1 teaspoon vegetable oil
5 garlic cloves, minced
1 pound ground beef
1 Tablespoon garlic powder
1 Tablespoon onion powder
½ teaspoon fine ground sea salt
½ cup water
1 cup frozen spinach, prepared according to package instructions
1-2 pieces lettuce per taco
½ cup Tzatziki (page 208)
Tortillas

Directions:

1. Heat vegetable oil in a medium frying pan over medium heat. Cook garlic until just turning brown, about 2 minutes.
2. Add ground beef to garlic and brown, about 8-10 minutes. Add garlic powder, onion powder, salt, and water, reduce heat to low, and simmer until water evaporates, about 8 more minutes.
3. Add cooked spinach, mix well, and cook 2 more minutes.
4. Cover a tortilla with lettuce, and top with beef and spinach mixture. Add at least a Tablespoon of Tzatziki.

Navajo Taco

The Navajo Taco is nothing more than a Classic American Taco on a fried, puffy tortilla, often called frybread, and is best served with a fork! To create one, simply follow the recipe for the Classic American Taco (page 6) and use a Navajo Taco Tortilla (page 148) instead of a standard tortilla. Navajo Taco Tortillas are much heavier in your stomach than traditional tortillas, so you will probably only want to eat one or two of these at a meal, especially if there are side dishes!

Philly Cheesesteak Taco

Sometimes you just have to have a cheesesteak, and now you can have one without the roll. Feel free to customize with mushrooms, hot peppers, or anything else you need on your cheesesteak!

Makes 4 tacos.
1 Tablespoon vegetable oil
1 medium onion, sliced
1 green pepper, thinly sliced
Butter for greasing
4 strips thinly sliced round roast, or frozen cheesesteak meat, thawed
8 slices provolone cheese
Coarse ground sea salt
Cracked black pepper
Salsa for topping, optional
Tortillas

DIRECTIONS:

1. Heat oil in a medium pan. Add onion and pepper slices to hot oil and sauté until tender, about 8-10 minutes.
2. Grease a griddle with butter and warm over medium heat. Place meat in flat strips on a hot griddle (a flat-bottom frying pan will do almost as well) and cook about 1 minute on each side until brown, but not done. Use two forks to shred strips into smaller pieces, keeping the piles from the 4 original strips separate. Cover each pile with 2 pieces of provolone cheese and let melt over meat. Toss gently as cheese melts to spread throughout meat.
3. Serve on a tortilla with peppers and onions. Add salt and pepper to taste, and top with a Tablespoon of salsa if desired.

Reuben Taco

A classic Reuben is typically served with Thousand Island dressing, but try Taco Russian Dressing here for fuller flavor.

Makes 4 tacos.
¼ cup Taco Russian Dressing (page 200)
1 cup sauerkraut, prepared
4 slices Swiss cheese
1 cup shredded corned beef, prepared
Cracked black pepper for garnish
Tortillas

Directions:
1. Preheat oven to 400°F.
2. Spread about 1 Tablespoon Taco Russian Dressing evenly over a tortilla.
3. Top with sauerkraut, 1 piece of swiss cheese, and corned beef.
4. Put taco on an oven-safe plate and heat 2-3 minutes until cheese melts. Garnish with cracked black pepper.

Santa Fe Taco Salad

Use leftover cooked beef from the Classic American Taco to make a salad for lunch the next day, or prepare a whole pound of beef to mix salads for a group!

Makes 1 salad.
2 cups iceberg lettuce, shredded
½ cup ground beef prepared as for Classic American Taco (page 6)
¼ cup shredded cheese (Mexican or taco blend)
½ cup Black Bean & Corn Salsa (page 178)
3-4 thin slices pepperjack cheese
½ lime per taco, for garnish
Taco Salad Bowl (page 150)

Directions:
1. Fill Taco Salad Bowl with lettuce. Top with beef, cheese, and Black Bean & Corn Salsa. Finish with cheese slices.
2. Serve with half a lime.

Traditional Taco Salad

Spice up the classic American taco ingredients by adding them to a baked Taco Salad Bowl and topping with Taco Salad Dressing for easy presentation that wows.

Makes 4 regular, or 2 large, taco salads.
½ pound ground beef
¼ cup water
1½ Tablespoons Classic Taco Seasoning (page 170)
½ head iceberg lettuce, shredded
1 medium tomato, diced
1 cup shredded cheese (Mexican or taco blend)
Taco Salad Dressing (page 202)
1 Taco Salad Bowl (page 150) per salad

DIRECTIONS:

1. Brown ground beef over medium-high heat, about 8-10 minutes. Add water and taco seasoning, and stir thoroughly. Cook 3 more minutes.
2. Add shredded lettuce to Taco Salad Bowl. Top with finished beef, using a slotted spoon to avoid grease from pan.
3. Add tomatoes and cheese and serve with Taco Salad Dressing on the side. Salsa works well as a dressing, too.

CHICKEN

Barbecue Chicken Taco
Chicken & Waffle Taco
Chicken Cacciatore Taco
Chicken Salad Taco
Chicken Tikka Taco
Chili Lime Chicken Taco
Chipotle Chicken Taco
Feta Chicken Taco
Grilled Chicken Taco
Orange Chicken Taco
Kurt's Pomegranate Chicken Taco
Southwestern Smoked Chicken Taco
Ian's Tomatillo Jam
Ian's Dry Rub

Barbecue Chicken Taco

Makes 6 tacos.
1 Tablespoon vegetable oil
2 boneless, skinless chicken breasts
1 can chicken broth (14.5 oz)
¼ cup Marsala cooking wine
¼ cup steak sauce
1 large tomato, diced
Kernels of 1 ear of corn, cut from cob
1 cup barbecue sauce
1 teaspoon black pepper
1 teaspoon fine ground sea salt
Tortillas

Directions:

1. Heat oil in a frying pan over medium heat. Add chicken breasts to pan and cook 3 minutes on each side.
2. While chicken is cooking, add broth, Marsala wine, and steak sauce to a Dutch oven, or other large pot that can be covered, and bring to a boil over medium-high heat. Reduce to simmer. When chicken is finished, add to liquid mixture and cover. Simmer 10 minutes.
3. Shred chicken into large pieces using two forks to pull meat apart. Pieces should become nearly submerged by liquid. Cover and cook 5 more minutes. Pull meat apart into smaller shreds, cover, and cook 5 more minutes.
4. With a slotted spoon, remove chicken to medium mixing bowl and add tomato, corn, barbecue sauce, pepper, and salt. Mix.
5. Serve on tortillas.

Chicken & Waffle Taco

Chicken & Waffles are the new salt and pepper; they are showing up together everywhere! Naturally, they make the perfect taco pairing.

Makes 6 tacos.
1 boneless, skinless chicken breast
¼ cup flour
¼ Tablespoon cornstarch
½ teaspoon garlic powder
¼ teaspoon chili powder
Dash of salt
¼ cup + 2 Tablespoons seltzer
1 cup panko bread crumbs
Vegetable oil for frying
2 waffles, cooked
½ cup maple syrup
Tortillas

Directions:

1. Cut chicken into strips, lengthwise, and set aside on plate; one chicken breast should yield about 6 strips.
2. Combine flour, cornstarch, garlic powder, chili powder, salt, and seltzer in a mixing bowl. Mix until there are no clumps remaining in the batter. Pour panko bread crumbs in another bowl.
3. Dredge a chicken strip in batter and drain excess. Strip should be only lightly battered, or bread crumbs will become clumpy. Dip battered strip in bread crumbs to coat, then return to plate. Repeat with all chicken strips.
4. Heat about an inch of vegetable oil in a frying pan and add chicken when hot, being careful not to crowd strips. (To test oil, wet a finger with water and flick a couple drops into the oil. If it sizzles, it is ready.) Cook 4-5 minutes, until golden brown on the outside and white on the inside.
5. Cut waffles into three strips each.
6. Top a tortilla with one strip of chicken and one strip of waffle. Drizzle maple syrup over taco.

Chicken Cacciatore Taco

Makes 6 tacos.
2 Tablespoons + 2 Tablespoons vegetable oil, separated
2 boneless, skinless chicken breasts
1 large onion, sliced thin
2 green peppers, sliced thin
4-6 cloves garlic (depending on preference), sliced thin
1 cup white wine
2 cups canned diced tomato with juices
½ teaspoon black pepper
1 teaspoon paprika
1 teaspoon dried oregano
1-2 whole lettuce leaves per taco
Tortillas

Directions:

1. Heat 2 Tablespoons oil in a Dutch oven over medium heat. Cut chicken into four quadrants per breast and lightly brown about 4 ½ minutes on each side. Remove chicken to a plate.
2. Add remaining 2 Tablespoons oil to the Dutch oven, raise the heat slightly to medium-high, and add onions and peppers. Cook until onions are soft, about 8 minutes, stirring several times. Add garlic and cook 1 minute more.
3. Add wine and scrape up brown bits from the bottom of the pan, and simmer until wine is reduced by half, about 10 minutes. Add tomatoes, pepper, paprika, and oregano, and cook 2 more minutes. Return chicken, cover, and simmer 25 minutes over low heat. Shred chicken with two forks.
4. Cover a tortilla with lettuce and top with cacciatore mixture. Use a slotted spoon to drain liquid and avoid a soggy taco.

Chicken Salad Taco

Makes 4 tacos.

1 Tablespoon vegetable oil
2 boneless, skinless chicken breasts
2 cans chicken broth (14.5 ounces each)
1 stalk celery, chopped
½ cup diced onion
4 Tablespoons mayonnaise
4 teaspoons mustard
2 teaspoons Classic Taco Seasoning (page 170)
4 teaspoons relish
1 teaspoon celery salt
Cracked black pepper to taste
1-2 pieces lettuce per taco
Tortillas

Directions:

1. Heat oil in a frying pan over medium heat. Add chicken breasts to pan and cook 3 minutes on each side.
2. While chicken is cooking, add broth to Dutch oven, or other large pot that can be covered, and bring to a boil over medium-high heat. Reduce to simmer. When chicken is ready, add to broth and cover. Simmer 10 minutes.
3. Shred chicken into large pieces using two forks to pull meat apart. Cover and cook 5 more minutes. Pull meat apart into smaller shreds, cover, and cook 5 more minutes.
4. Combine all remaining ingredients except lettuce and tortillas to medium mixing bowl with chicken and mix thoroughly.
5. Cover a tortilla with lettuce and top with chicken salad.

Chicken Tikka Taco

This wonderful taco is based on an Indian dish popularized in the UK and is sure to surprise anyone with its awesome flavor in this unexpected form. You can make your own tikka masala sauce, but this is one of the rare times I recommend purchasing a pre-made sauce to save a lot of time and effort.

Makes 6 tacos.

2 Tablespoons vegetable oil
2 boneless, skinless chicken breasts, chopped into bite-size pieces
1 Tablespoon curry powder (yellow)
½ Tablespoon butter
1 cup tikka masala sauce
⅓ cup heavy cream
1-2 whole pieces of lettuce per taco
2 large plum tomatoes, sliced long
Cracked black pepper for garnish
Tortillas

Directions:

1. Heat oil in a Dutch oven over medium heat. Add chicken pieces, sprinkle with curry, and lightly brown chicken, about 5-6 minutes, stirring almost constantly for even browning.
2. Meanwhile, in a small pot, melt butter over medium heat. Add tikka masala sauce and heavy cream, mix, and heat until mixture begins to boil. Remove from heat immediately and add to chicken. Cover and cook 20 minutes.
3. With a slotted spoon, remove chicken to a plate and cut into very small pieces (each bite-size piece should be reduced to about three smaller pieces). Reserve sauce.
4. Top a tortilla with lettuce. Add chicken, some tomato slices, and about a Tablespoon of the leftover sauce. Garnish with cracked black pepper.

**Any remaining sauce goes great over simple white rice, which is a perfect side for this taco!*

Chili Lime Chicken Taco

Makes 6 tacos.

1 Tablespoon vegetable oil
2 boneless, skinless chicken breasts
1 can chicken broth (14.5 oz)
Juice of two limes (about 2.5 oz)
½ Tablespoon red chili powder
1 Tablespoon dried oregano
Kernels of 1 ear of corn, cut from cob
1 cup Mild Salsa (page 194)
½ head iceberg lettuce, shredded
Fresh cilantro for garnish
Tortillas

Directions:

1. Heat oil in a frying pan over medium heat. Add chicken breasts to pan and cook 3 minutes on each side.
2. While chicken is cooking, add broth, lime juice, red chili powder, and oregano to Dutch oven, or other large pot that can be covered, and bring to a boil over medium-high heat. Reduce to simmer. When chicken is ready, add to liquid mixture and cover. Simmer 10 minutes.
3. Shred chicken into large pieces using two forks to pull meat apart. Pieces should become nearly submerged by liquid. Cover and cook 5 more minutes. Pull meat apart into smaller shreds, cover, and cook 5 more minutes.
4. With a slotted spoon, remove chicken to medium mixing bowl and add corn and salsa. Mix.
5. Serve on tortillas over shredded lettuce and garnish with fresh cilantro.

Chipotle Chicken Taco

Makes 4 tacos.
1 Tablespoon vegetable oil
2 boneless, skinless chicken breasts
2 cans chicken broth (14.5 ounces each)
1 cup Chipotle Salsa (page 182)
Sour cream for topping, if desired
Tortillas

DIRECTIONS:

1. Heat oil in a frying pan over medium heat. Add chicken breasts to pan and cook 3 minutes on each side.
2. While chicken is cooking, add broth to Dutch oven, or other large pot that can be covered, and bring to a boil over medium-high heat. Reduce to simmer. When chicken is ready, add to broth and cover. Simmer 10 minutes.
3. Shred chicken into large pieces using two forks to pull meat apart. Cover and cook 5 more minutes. Pull meat apart into smaller shreds, cover, and cook 5 more minutes.
4. Combine chicken and Chipotle Salsa in a medium mixing bowl and mix well.
5. Place on a tortilla. Top with sour cream, if desired.

Feta Chicken Taco

Makes 6 tacos.

1 Tablespoon + 1 teaspoon vegetable oil, separated
2 boneless, skinless chicken breasts
1 can chicken broth (14.5 ounces)
1 small onion, sliced
1 medium hot pepper, seeded and sliced
1 scant teaspoon fine ground sea salt
4 heaping Tablespoons feta cheese + more for topping
2 teaspoons adobo seasoning
Cracked black pepper for topping
Tortillas

Directions:

1. Heat 1 Tablespoon oil in a frying pan over medium heat. Add chicken breasts to pan and cook 3 minutes on each side.
2. While chicken is cooking, add broth to Dutch oven, or other large pot that can be covered, and bring to a boil over medium-high heat. Reduce to simmer. When chicken is ready, add to broth and cover. Simmer 10 minutes.
3. Meanwhile, heat remaining oil in a small pan over medium-high heat. Add onions, hot pepper, and salt, and cook until tender, about 8-10 minutes.
4. After 10 minutes of cooking, shred chicken into large pieces using two forks to pull meat apart. Pieces should become nearly submerged by liquid. Cover and cook 5 more minutes. Pull meat apart into smaller shreds, cover, and cook 5 more minutes.
5. Add shredded chicken, onion, hot pepper, 4 heaping Tablespoons feta cheese, and adobo seasoning to a medium mixing bowl, and mix thoroughly.
6. Add chicken mixture to a tortilla and top with cracked black pepper and a sprinkling of feta cheese.

Grilled Chicken Taco

Makes 6 tacos.
1 Tablespoon vegetable oil
2 boneless, skinless chicken breasts
1½ Tablespoons Spicy Grill Rub (page 172)
½ head iceberg lettuce, shredded
1 medium tomato, diced
1½ cups shredded cheese (Mexican or taco blend)
Taco Sauce (page 204) for topping
Sour cream for topping
½ lime per taco, for garnish
Tortillas

Directions:

1. Preheat oven to 400°F.
2. Heat vegetable oil in frying pan over medium heat. Cover one side of chicken with Spicy Grill Rub, and cook chicken, seasoned side up for 4½ minutes. Flip and cook 4½ more minutes. Wrap handle in aluminum foil and move pan to preheated oven. Cook for 8-9 minutes, or until chicken is no longer pink in the center. Remove to a plate or cutting board to cool, about 5 minutes.
3. Slice chicken into thin strips and serve atop shredded lettuce on a tortilla. Top with tomato, cheese, taco sauce, and sour cream. Serve with half a lime.

Orange Chicken Taco

Chinese food on a taco? Absolutely! Make your own orange chicken for a healthier version to Chinese takeout, then put it on a tortilla over lettuce for a fantastic Asian taco!

Makes 2 tacos.
2½ cups water
¼ cup orange juice
⅓ cup rice vinegar
2 Tablespoons soy sauce
⅔ cup brown sugar
1 teaspoon garlic powder
1 teaspoon ginger powder
1 boneless, skinless chicken breast
1 cup flour
½ teaspoon salt
½ teaspoon black pepper
2 Tablespoons vegetable oil
3 Tablespoons cornstarch
2 Tablespoons water
1-2 pieces lettuce per taco
Garlic Ginger Tortillas (page 146)

DIRECTIONS:

1. Combine water, orange juice, rice vinegar, soy sauce, brown sugar, garlic powder, and ginger powder in a medium pan over medium-high heat. Bring to a boil, stirring to dissolve sugar, then turn off heat and cool 15 minutes.
2. Cut chicken into ½-inch chunks, place in a sealable bag, and add 1 cup cool orange sauce. Reserve remaining sauce. Refrigerate chicken and reserved sauce at least 1 hour, preferably overnight.
3. Using a slotted spoon, remove chicken chunks to a plate lined with paper towels. In another sealable bag, add flour, salt, pepper, and marinated chicken chunks. Shake to coat.
4. Add vegetable oil to a medium pan over medium-high heat. Brown coated chicken chunks on all sides, about 4-6 minutes. Drizzle extra oil over chicken chunks if pan becomes too dry.
5. Combine cornstarch and water in a small mixing bowl and mix until no chunks remain. Add to reserved orange sauce, then add to chicken chunks. Cook 5 more minutes.
6. Cover a tortilla with lettuce and top with orange chicken.

Kurt's Pomegranate Chicken Taco

A delicious creation by R. Kurt Osenlund, inspired by my favorite Middle Eastern salad with a spice change and added chicken, this taco tastes great hot or cold.

Makes 4 tacos.
1 Tablespoon vegetable oil
2 boneless, skinless chicken breasts
2 cans chicken broth (14.5 ounces each)
2 plum tomatoes, sliced and halved (half moons)
2 Tablespoons olive oil
1 teaspoon fine ground sea salt
2 teaspoons coriander powder
½ cup pomegranate seeds + some for topping
Tortillas

DIRECTIONS:

1. Heat oil in a frying pan over medium heat. Add chicken breasts to pan and cook 3 minutes on each side.
2. While chicken is cooking, add broth to Dutch oven, or other large pot that can be covered, and bring to a boil over medium-high heat. Reduce to simmer. When chicken is ready, add to broth and cover. Simmer 10 minutes.
3. Shred chicken into large pieces using two forks to pull meat apart. Cover and cook 5 more minutes. Pull meat apart into smaller shreds, cover, and cook 5 more minutes.
4. Combine tomato, olive oil, salt, coriander, and ½ cup pomegranate seeds in a medium mixing bowl. Let sit 5 minutes.
5. Add chicken and mix thoroughly.
6. Top a tortilla with chicken mixture. Top with remaining pomegranate seeds.

Southwestern Smoked Chicken Taco

Chicken and Gouda bring a deep, smoky flavor complemented by tangy barbecue sauce, and tomatillo jam adds a nice sweetness and some well-hidden heat to this recipe, created by culinary enthusiast Ian Skuse.

Makes 8-10 tacos.

2 cups water, or enough to cover chicken
3 Tablespoons salt
5 chicken thighs (bone-in with skin)
Applewood chips
¼ cup mustard
Ian's Dry Rub (page 47), enough to cover chicken
¼ cup barbecue sauce
Smoked Gouda (shredded)
Ian's Tomatillo Jam (page 46) for topping
Barbecue sauce for topping
1 cup halved grape tomatoes
1 avocado, chopped into medium chunks
Tortillas

DIRECTIONS:

1. Combine water and salt and mix until salt dissolves. Pour into a baking dish large enough to hold chicken. Add chicken to the brine, covered with plastic wrap, for a minimum of 1 hour, preferably overnight.
2. Soak applewood chips in water for about 30 minutes. Set a meat smoker to 240°F.
3. Remove chicken from brine and rinse well. On a cookie sheet, pat the chicken dry and lightly brush both sides with mustard. Coat with Ian's Dry Rub. Place the chicken skin side down, wrap the skin securely around, and hold closed with toothpicks.
4. Drain applewood chips and add to smoker. Add chicken thighs. Cook for about 2 hours and 15 minutes, until internal temperature reaches 165°F. Remove thighs and coat with barbecue sauce, then return to smoker for another 15 minutes.
5. Remove chicken and let rest 5-10 minutes, covered with foil. Slice or pull apart into pieces.
6. Add chicken to tortillas with shredded Gouda, Ian's Tomatillo Jam, and a drizzle of barbecue sauce. Top with tomato and avocado.

Shown here without Ian's Tomatillo Jam

Ian's Tomatillo Jam

Makes about 12 ounces.

4 medium tomatillos, diced, cores removed
1 medium tomato, diced, core removed
5 Turkish hot baby peppers or 1 jalapeno, sliced with seeds
1½ cups sugar
¼ teaspoon pectin

Directions:

1. Combine tomatillos, tomato, pepper(s), and sugar in a medium pan, and set over medium-high heat. When sugar dissolves into liquid, set to high heat and bring contents to a boil. Stir about 8-10 minutes until slightly thickened. Set heat to medium-low and simmer for about an hour, until jam thickens.
2. Add pectin and mix well.
3. Remove to heat-safe container and set aside to cool.

Ian's Dry Rub

Use this dry rub recipe on smoked meats to be used in tacos, and skip the taco seasoning for a deeper flavor alternative to the traditional taco.

1 cup salt
1 cup brown sugar
½ cup paprika
¼ cup garlic powder
¼ cup chili powder
½ cup black pepper
2 teaspoons ground mustard

Directions:
1. Mix all ingredients in a bowl, and store in a spice jar or other airtight container.

Baja Fish Taco
California Roll Taco
Smoked Salmon Taco
Tuna Salad Taco

Baja Fish Taco

Makes 2 tacos.
6 oz filet white fish (cod)
¼ cup flour
¼ Tablespoon cornstarch
½ teaspoon garlic powder
¼ teaspoon chili powder
Dash of salt
¼ cup + 2 Tablespoons seltzer
1 cup panko bread crumbs
Vegetable oil for frying
1 Tablespoon Baja Taco Sauce (page 176) per taco
¼ cup shredded cabbage
½ avocado, sliced
Mango Salsa (page 186) for topping
Tortillas

DIRECTIONS:

1. Cut fish into strips no more than 1 inch wide and 2 inches long. Set aside on plate.
2. Combine flour, cornstarch, garlic powder, chili powder, salt, and seltzer in a mixing bowl. Mix until there are no clumps remaining in the batter. Pour panko bread crumbs in another bowl.
3. Dredge a fish strip in batter and drain excess. Strip should be only lightly battered, or bread crumbs will become clumpy. Dip battered strip in bread crumbs to coat, then return to plate. Repeat with all fish strips.
4. Heat about a half inch of vegetable oil in a frying pan and add fish when hot. (To test oil, wet a finger with water and flick a couple drops into the oil. If it sizzles, it is ready.) Cook 2½ minutes. Flip and cook another 2 minutes.
5. Spread 1 Tablespoon Baja Taco Sauce evenly on tortilla. Top with 2-3 fish pieces (too many and the taco will not close!), shredded cabbage, and a few avocado slices. Top with Mango Salsa.

California Roll Taco

Be careful not to add soy sauce before serving or the taco will become soggy and impossible to hold; serve it on the side for dipping or for drizzling immediately prior to eating.

Makes 3-4 tacos.
2 oz crab meat
1 small cucumber
¼ avocado
1 cup cooked Japanese rice (sometimes called sushi rice); basmati works well, too
Wasabi sauce (or wasabi paste, if preferred) for topping
Soy sauce for dipping
Tortillas

Directions:

1. Cut crab meat, cucumber, and avocado into thin matchsticks, no more than three inches long. (To make the cucumber more manageable, cut the rounded edges off of four sides to make a long rectangle that sits flat on the work surface, then cut into strips. You will need to be a little creative with the avocado to make strips.)
2. Add about ¼ cup of rice to a tortilla, gently patting down with the back of a spoon. Top with 3-4 pieces each of crab, cucumber, and avocado.
3. Drizzle wasabi sauce on top and serve with a side of soy sauce.

Smoked Salmon Taco

Makes 2 tacos.
3 Tablespoons cream cheese, softened
1 scant teaspoon paprika
½ teaspoon cumin
1 teaspoon chopped dill
¼ pound smoked salmon
1 scant Tablespoon capers, drained
Several very thin slices red onion
Dill for garnish
Cracked pepper for garnish
Tortillas

DIRECTIONS:

1. Combine cream cheese, paprika, cumin, and dill in a small mixing bowl. Top tortilla with a thin layer of this sauce.
2. Add smoked salmon, capers, and a few slices of red onion.
3. Top with dill and black pepper.

Tuna Salad Taco

Makes 2 tacos.

1 can of tuna in water, drained
2 Tablespoons red onion, chopped
¼ cup celery, chopped
1 Tablespoon mayonnaise
1 teaspoon Taco Mustard (page 198)
1-2 pieces lettuce per taco
Paprika for garnish
Cracked black pepper for garnish
Tortillas

DIRECTIONS:

1. Combine tuna, red onion, celery, mayonnaise, and Taco Mustard in a medium mixing bowl and mix thoroughly.
2. Cover a tortilla with lettuce and top with tuna salad.
3. Garnish with paprika and black pepper.

PORK

Barbecue Pork Taco
BLT Taco
Hawaiian Pork Taco
New Year's Taco
Pork Carnitas
Sausage & Peppers Taco

Barbecue Pork Taco

Makes 6-8 tacos.

1 Tablespoon butter
1 medium white onion, sliced
2 pounds pork, cut into 7 or 8 large chunks
2 cans vegetable broth (14.5 oz each)
1½ cups barbecue sauce
1 teaspoon black pepper
2 cups lettuce, torn into large pieces
1 large tomato, diced
1 Tablespoon sour cream per taco
Tortillas

Directions:

1. Melt butter in a Dutch oven over medium-high heat. Add onion and sauté until tender, about 6-7 minutes. Add pork and brown on all sides, about 10 minutes. Add vegetable broth and bring to a boil. Reduce to a simmer, cover, and cook 1 hour.
2. Shred pork into large pieces using two forks to pull meat apart. Cover and cook 10 more minutes. Pull meat apart into smaller shreds, cover, and cook 10 more minutes. Strain.
3. In a medium mixing bowl, mix pork, barbecue sauce, and pepper.
4. Loosely cover a tortilla with torn lettuce. Top with pork, tomato, and sour cream.

BLT Taco

Makes 2 tacos.
4 strips bacon
2 heaping Tablespoons Taco Aioli (page 196)
1 cup lettuce, shredded
1 plum tomato, sliced thin, then cut in strips
Shredded cheese (Mexican or taco blend) for garnish
Tortillas

Directions:

1. Fry bacon in an ungreased pan over medium heat until crispy, about 10 minutes. Remove to plate, lined with paper towel, to cool. Tear into long, thin pieces when cool.
2. Spread a heaping Tablespoon of Taco Aioli on a tortilla and top with a bed of shredded lettuce. Add a few tomato strips and the pieces of one strip of bacon. Top with a light sprinkling of cheese for color.

Hawaiian Pork Taco

Makes 6-8 tacos.
1 Tablespoon butter
1 medium white onion, sliced
2 pounds pork, cut into 7 or 8 large chunks
2 cans vegetable broth (14.5 oz each)
½ cup crushed pineapple, drained well
1 can white beans (15 oz)
2-3 leaves green lettuce per taco
Tortillas

Directions:

1. Melt butter in a Dutch oven over medium-high heat. Add onion and sauté until tender, about 6-7 minutes. Add pork and brown on all sides, about 10 minutes. Add vegetable broth and bring to a boil. Reduce to a simmer, cover, and cook 1 hour.
2. Shred pork into large pieces using two forks to pull meat apart. Cover and cook 10 more minutes. Pull meat apart into smaller shreds, cover, and cook 10 more minutes. Strain.
3. In a medium mixing bowl, mix pork, pineapple, and beans.
4. Place 2-3 whole lettuce leaves on a tortilla and top with pork mixture.

New Year's Taco

Try this taco for a fun take on the traditional New Year's Day pork and sauerkraut dinner.

Makes 6-8 tacos.
1 Tablespoon butter
1 medium white onion, sliced
2 pounds pork, cut into 7 or 8 large chunks
2 cans vegetable broth (14.5 oz each)
1 pound sauerkraut
½ teaspoon celery salt
1 Tablespoon brown sugar
1 cup Taco Mustard (page 198)
Dried oregano for garnish
Paprika for garnish
Cracked black pepper for garnish
Tortillas

Directions:

1. Melt butter in a Dutch oven over medium-high heat. Add onion and sauté until tender, about 6-7 minutes. Add pork and brown on all sides, about 10 minutes. Add vegetable broth and bring to a boil. Reduce to a simmer, cover, and cook 1 hour.
2. Shred pork into large pieces using two forks to pull meat apart. Cover and cook 10 more minutes. Pull meat apart into smaller shreds, cover, and cook 10 more minutes. Strain.
3. Add sauerkraut, celery salt, and brown sugar to a medium saucepan over medium heat. Stir well and cook until hot, about 5-6 minutes. Strain.
4. Spread about 1 teaspoon of Taco Mustard on a tortilla. Top with pork and sauerkraut. Garnish with seasonings.

Pork Carnitas

The pork carnita is a hall-of-famer that too often comes out dry and underwhelming when prepared at home, or even at sub-par restaurants. This recipe guarantees a moist, savory taco without a ton of work, and practically makes its own side dish in the process!

Makes 10 tacos.

¼ cup bacon grease or vegetable oil
2 pounds pork shoulder, chopped in 7-8 large chunks
2 Tablespoons fine ground sea salt
3 large cloves garlic, crushed
1 Tablespoon red chili powder
1 teaspoon oregano
1½ teaspoons cumin
Juice of 1 lime
2 small cans chicken broth (14.5 oz each)
2 cups shredded lettuce
3 tomatoes, diced
Fresh cilantro for garnish
½ lime per plate
Tortillas

Directions:

1. Heat bacon grease or vegetable oil in a Dutch oven over high heat. Bacon grease adds depth to the final flavor, but vegetable oil works well, too. Season pork with salt, then add to the Dutch oven and brown on all sides, 10-12 minutes. Add remaining dry ingredients, followed by lime juice and chicken broth. Bring to a boil. Reduce heat to low, cover, and simmer until pork is extremely tender, 2½ hours.
2. Place pork in a deep baking dish, drizzle with a ladle of juice from the Dutch oven, and bake at 400°F for 30 minutes, stopping twice to shred pork with two forks and add more juice. Be sure to withhold at least two ladles of juice if you are making Carnitas Rice.
3. Top a tortilla with shredded lettuce, pork, tomato, and cilantro. Serve with half a lime and extra cilantro for added flavor.

Serve with: Carnitas Rice (page 156), made with the leftover juices from Pork Carnitas!

Sausage & Peppers Taco

Serve this with a simple green salad tossed with olive oil and vinegar for a light, yet hearty, Italian spin on the taco.

Makes 12 tacos.
1 large red pepper
1 large green pepper
1 medium onion
1 pound mild Italian sausage
1 teaspoon black pepper
1 Tablespoon vegetable oil
1 can diced tomato (14 oz)
Tortillas

Directions:
1. Julienne the vegetables, leaving the onions slightly thicker, and set aside.
2. Remove the casing from the sausage and place in a large frying pan over medium heat. Use two forks to pull it apart as it browns, creating chunks no larger than one inch, the crumblier the better. Add black pepper and cook until completely browned, about 8 minutes, stirring frequently. Remove sausage and juices to a bowl.
3. Add vegetables to pan over medium heat, top with vegetable oil and sauté until soft, about 10 minutes.
4. Add diced tomato and cook for 2 minutes.
5. Return sausage to vegetables and cook 5 minutes.
6. Serve on tortillas, using tongs to avoid excess tomato juice or tacos will become soggy.

VEGETABLE

California Tofu Taco
Caprese Taco
Falafel Tahini Taco
Korean Taco
Potato Taco (taco de papa)
Roasted Vegetable Taco
Root Vegetable Taco
Steamed Broccoli Taco
Three-Bean Taco
Turkish Soft Potato Taco
Vegetable Stir Fry Taco
Waldorf Taco
Zucchini Pesto Taco

California Tofu Taco

Makes 4 tacos.
¼ cup Avocado Spread (page 174)
1 piece of lettuce per taco
3 ounces tofu, sliced in strips
1 avocado, peeled and chopped
½ small red onion, sliced thin
Tortillas

Directions:
1. Cover a tortilla with an even layer of Avocado Spread and top with lettuce.
2. Add tofu, avocado, and red onion.

Caprese Taco

Turn this classic Italian salad into a taco appetizer before an Italian meal or an Italian-themed taco entree. For an even more Italian feel, slide the tortilla out from under the taco and use it as bread to accompany the salad after serving!

Makes 2 tacos.
1 cup tomato, julienned
1 cup mozzarella, julienned
2 teaspoons olive oil
1½ teaspoons cumin
1½ teaspoons balsamic vinegar
Dash of fine ground sea salt
1-2 pieces lettuce per taco
Basil, torn, for topping
Tortillas

Directions:

1. Mix all ingredients except lettuce, basil, and tortillas in a medium mixing bowl and allow to sit at least 2 minutes.
2. Meanwhile, heat a cast-iron skillet over medium-high heat. Heat a tortilla 1 extra minute on each side until slightly firm, then top with lettuce and tomato mixture. Finish with basil.

Shown here with purple basil.

Falafel Tahini Taco

Makes 4-6 tacos.

1 package falafel mix (7 ounces)
1-2 pieces lettuce per taco
1 plum tomato, diced
½ cucumber, sliced very thin
¼ cup Tahini (page 206)
2 Tablespoons water
2 Tablespoons olive oil
Dash of salt
Tortillas

Directions:

1. Prepare falafel according to package instructions. When cool, halve falafel balls.
2. Cover a tortilla with lettuce. Add about 6 falafel halves, tomato, and cucumber.
3. In a small mixing bowl, combine tahini, water, olive oil, and salt, and mix well. Drizzle on top of finished taco.

Korean Taco

Makes 4-6 tacos.
¾ cup uncooked white rice
1 jar kimchi (14 ounces)
Cracked black pepper for garnish
Garlic Ginger Tortillas (page 146)

Directions:

1. Prepare rice according to package directions.
2. Top a Garlic Ginger Tortilla with a thin layer of cooked rice, gently patted down. Add kimchi and top with freshly cracked black pepper.

Potato Taco (taco de papa)

Makes 4 tacos.

1 small hot pepper (as hot as you like it), seeded
2 Tablespoons olive oil
2 cups red potato, peeled and diced in ½-inch cubes
½ cup green pepper, diced
½ cup fresh corn kernels (canned whole kernels, well drained, will work)
4 cloves garlic, minced
Salt and black pepper to taste
Juice of 1 small lime
½ cup sour cream
1 small avocado, cubed
½ cup torn cilantro
Tortillas

Directions:

1. Heat cast-iron skillet over medium-high heat until hot. Slice hot pepper and sear, cut-side down, about 4 minutes. Remove to cutting board to cool.
2. Reduce heat to medium and add olive oil to skillet. When hot, add potatoes and cook until golden brown and starting to blacken, about 10-12 minutes. Remove to a plate lined with paper towel to dry.
3. If skillet is completely dry, add a teaspoon of olive oil. Otherwise, simply add green pepper, corn, garlic, salt, pepper, and lime juice to skillet and cook 4-5 minutes, until corn begins to blacken and peppers become slightly tender.
4. Add a teaspoon of sour cream to the center of a tortilla and pat down gently. Top with potato and vegetable mixture. Top with avocado and garnish with cilantro.

Roasted Vegetable Taco

Makes 4-6 tacos.
1 teaspoon vegetable oil
½ zucchini, sliced in circles, then halved
½ squash, sliced in circles, then halved
½ small eggplant, sliced in circles, then halved (in thirds as circles get toward fat end)
5 cloves garlic, halved
1 Tablespoon Classic Taco Seasoning (page 170)
½ cup Taco Aioli (page 196)
Tortillas

DIRECTIONS:

1. Preheat oven to 375°F.
2. Grease a baking pan lightly with oil and arrange vegetable pieces (including garlic) so they do not overlap. Sprinkle with Classic Taco Seasoning. Cook 10 minutes. Toss gently with a spatula (they can overlap now) and cook an additional 7 minutes.
3. Top a tortilla with 1 Tablespoon of Taco Aioli, spread evenly. Add vegetables.

Root Vegetable Taco

The variety of spices in this vegetarian taco, from the depth of the garam masala to the dessert quality of the nutmeg, combine for a full flavor experience that will satisfy anyone. This is an easy one to prepare for large groups; as taco filling, the vegetables taste just as good at room temperature as they do hot!

Makes 4-6 tacos.

4 medium carrots, peeled
2 large parsnips, peeled
¼ cup olive oil
½ cup butter (one stick)
1 teaspoon paprika
1 teaspoon garam masala
1 teaspoon nutmeg
1 teaspoon Classic Taco Seasoning (page 170)
Dash of fine ground sea salt
1-2 pieces lettuce per taco
1 Tablespoon sour cream per taco
Paprika for garnish
Tortillas

DIRECTIONS:

1. Preheat oven to 400°F.
2. Slice carrots and parsnips in ¼-inch sticks, about 4 inches long. Place vegetables on a parchment paper-lined baking sheet, drizzle with olive oil (you may not use all of it), and roast for 15 minutes.
3. Melt butter in a small pot over medium heat. Add paprika, garam masala, nutmeg, Classic Taco Seasoning, and salt, and stir.
4. When vegetables are finished, spoon seasoned butter over vegetables. Return to oven and cook 10 more minutes. With tongs, remove to a plate to cool and dry 2-3 minutes.
5. Cover tortilla with lettuce, top with vegetables, and add a Tablespoon of sour cream. Garnish with paprika.

Steamed Broccoli Taco

A simple, refreshing vegetarian taco with an Asian flair.

Makes 2 tacos.
2 cups chopped broccoli
1 teaspoon olive oil
4 cloves garlic, chopped
1 Tablespoon + 2 Tablespoons soy sauce, separated
Garlic Ginger Tortillas (page 146)

DIRECTIONS:

1. Bring water in a steamer to a rolling boil, then steam broccoli 5 minutes. Remove to a medium mixing bowl immediately to prevent further cooking.
2. While broccoli is steaming, heat olive oil in a small pan over medium-high heat. Add garlic cloves and cook until turning brown, about 2-3 minutes. Add 1 Tablespoon soy sauce, turn off heat, and mix until soy sauce is absorbed/evaporated, about 20-30 seconds.
3. Combine garlic with broccoli in mixing bowl and add remaining 2 Tablespoons soy sauce. Mix well.
4. Use two Garlic Ginger Tortillas and top with broccoli and garlic, using a slotted spoon to prevent excess soy sauce from weakening tortillas; two are recommended to withstand remaining soy sauce, or tortillas may crumble easily.

Note: This taco also works well with lettuce wraps instead of tortillas, but add some grated fresh ginger in this case to make up for the flavor lost with the tortilla.

Three-Bean Taco

Makes 6 tacos.
1 can (15 oz) black beans
1 can (15 oz) great northern white beans
1 can (15 oz) red kidney beans
2 Tablespoons olive oil
1 Tablespoon dried oregano
1 scant Tablespoon black pepper
½ Tablespoon fine ground sea salt
1 cup lettuce, shredded
1 plum tomato, diced
Tortillas

Directions:
1. Drain beans well and mix in a large mixing bowl.
2. Pour half of the mixture into a food processor, add the olive oil, oregano, pepper, and salt, and blend until smooth.
3. Spread 1-2 Tablespoons of blended bean mix over tortilla. Add whole beans, a few pieces of lettuce, and a few pieces of tomato.

Turkish Soft Potato Taco

Makes 4-6 tacos.

2 cups peeled, diced potato (about 2 large potatoes cut in ½-inch cubes)
1 teaspoon cumin
½ teaspoon turmeric
½ teaspoon paprika
1½ cups Chickpea & White Bean Hummus (page 180)
1-2 pieces lettuce per taco
1 cup sour cream
Salsa for topping, if desired
Tortillas

DIRECTIONS:

1. Place potato cubes in boiling water, return to a full boil, and cook 2 minutes. Drain. Add cumin, turmeric, and paprika, and toss gently.
2. Heat a cast-iron skillet or heavy pan until very hot, then add potatoes and brown, stirring often but gently, about 10 minutes, until potatoes begin to turn gold and black in specs. Allow to cool at least 3 minutes.
3. Top a tortilla with 1½ Tablespoons Chickpea & White Bean Hummus. Add lettuce and sour cream, patted down gently. Top with potatoes. Add a Tablespoon of salsa for extra flavor, if desired.

Vegetable Stir Fry Taco

Makes 4-6 tacos.

1 small red pepper, sliced
1 small green pepper, sliced
1 medium onion, sliced thin
1 cup chopped broccoli
1 small carrot, shredded
2 Tablespoons + 1 teaspoon olive oil, separated
½ teaspoon powdered ginger
3 Tablespoons soy sauce
1-2 pieces lettuce per taco
Garlic Ginger Tortillas (page 146)

Directions:

1. Combine vegetables in a large mixing bowl and toss with 2 Tablespoons olive oil and powdered ginger.
2. Heat a large pan over medium-high heat and add remaining 1 teaspoon olive oil. When oil is hot, reduce heat to low, add vegetables, and cook until vegetables are tender with a slight crunch, about 15 minutes.
3. Add soy sauce and cook 1½ additional minutes, uncovered.
4. Top Garlic Ginger Tortilla with lettuce, and add vegetables.

Waldorf Taco

Try asking someone to list the ingredients of a true Waldorf salad and you will get all sorts of responses, including lettuce, which is not one of the original ingredients! This taco has been whittled down to reflect the true Waldorf, and it is delicious!

Makes 4 tacos.
½ apple, any variety, sliced thin
½ celery stick, chopped
¼ cup walnuts, crushed
¼ cup Taco Mayonnaise (page 197)
Tortillas

Directions:
1. Toss apple, celery, and walnuts in a small mixing bowl.
2. Top a tortilla with an even layer of Taco Mayonnaise. Add apple mixture.

Zucchini Pesto Taco

Makes 2 tacos.
1 zucchini
1 Tablespoon Pesto (page 188)
Pinch of coarse ground sea salt per taco, for garnish
Cracked black pepper, for garnish
Tortillas

Directions:
1. Peel zucchini, then use a julienne peeler to shred into "pasta."
2. Add zucchini pasta and pesto to a small mixing bowl, and toss with two forks to cover pasta with pesto.
3. Top a tortilla with pesto zucchini and garnish with salt and pepper.

BREAKFAST

Bacon, Egg & Cheese Taco
Black & Blue Breakfast Taco
Mexican Scrambled Egg Taco
Southwestern Omelet Taco
Strawberry Vanilla Breakfast Taco
Tropical Fruit Taco

Bacon, Egg & Cheese Taco

Turn a classic American breakfast sandwich into a taco with this recipe for a rich flavor that will satisfy any bacon lover.

Makes 2 tacos.
2 strips of bacon
3 eggs
1 Tablespoon milk
1 teaspoon dried oregano
½ teaspoon black pepper
½ teaspoon garlic powder
½ teaspoon red chili powder
¼ teaspoon fine ground sea salt
¼ cup shredded cheese (Mexican or taco blend)
Shredded cheese for garnish, if desired
Tortillas

Directions:

1. Fry bacon in an ungreased pan over medium heat until crispy, about 10 minutes. Reserve 1 Tablespoon of bacon grease.
2. Meanwhile, beat eggs with all remaining ingredients except tortillas in a small bowl. Heat reserved bacon grease in a small pan over medium heat and add egg mixture when hot. Crumble bacon and scatter evenly atop eggs. When bottom of eggs are firm, fold in half (as if making an omelet) and heat another 2 minutes. Unfold to a full, solid circle. (If eggs seal shut in some places, slide a spatula through and they will separate easily.)
3. Cut eggs in half and serve on warm tortillas with the straight edge of the eggs in the center for easy folding. Top with more shredded cheese, if desired.

Black & Blue Breakfast Taco

Makes 4 tacos.

1 cup vanilla yogurt
1 teaspoon brown sugar
¼ cup blueberries, partially mashed
1 cup blackberries
Brown Sugar Tortillas (page 140)

DIRECTIONS:

1. Mix yogurt, brown sugar, and blueberries.
2. Spread about 1½ Tablespoons yogurt mix on a tortilla. Top with a line of blackberries toward one end and roll as tightly as possible without breaking.
3. Serve upside down to hold roll closed.

Mexican Scrambled Egg Taco

To add some kick to this simple Mexican breakfast-turned-taco, add half of a sliced chili pepper (no seeds!) when cooking the eggs.

Makes 2 tacos.
1 Tablespoon vegetable oil
1 small onion, diced (about ½ cup)
3 eggs
1 Tablespoon milk
½ teaspoon fine ground sea salt
1 small plum tomato, diced (about ½ cup)
½ chili pepper, minced, if desired
Tortillas
Salsa for topping (page 192 or 194)

Directions:

1. Heat vegetable oil in a small pan over medium heat. Add onions and cook until soft and beginning to brown, 4-5 minutes. Add chili pepper, if desired.
2. Meanwhile, beat eggs, milk, and salt in a small bowl. Add to onions along with tomatoes and cook to desired consistency, stirring constantly.
3. Serve with warm tortillas and a side of salsa for topping!

Southwestern Omelet Taco

Makes 2 tacos.
1 teaspoon vegetable oil
½ small onion, diced
½ green pepper, diced
3 eggs
1 Tablespoon milk
½ teaspoon black pepper
½ teaspoon garlic powder
½ teaspoon red chili powder
¼ teaspoon fine ground sea salt
¼ cup shredded cheese (Mexican or taco blend)
¼ cup Mild Salsa (page 194), plus more for serving
Shredded cheese for garnish, if desired
Tortillas

Directions:

1. Heat vegetable oil in a medium pan over medium-high heat. Add onion and green pepper and cook until tender, about 6-8 minutes.
2. Meanwhile, beat eggs with all remaining ingredients except tortillas in a small bowl. When bottom of eggs are firm, fold in half (as if making an omelet) and heat another 2 minutes. Unfold to a full, solid circle. (If eggs seal shut in some places, slide a spatula through and they will separate easily.)
3. Cut eggs in half and serve on warm tortillas with the straight edge of the eggs in the center for easy folding. Top with more shredded cheese, if desired.
4. Serve with more salsa on the side.

Strawberry Vanilla Breakfast Taco

Maybe a breakfast taco, maybe a dessert taco. You decide!

Makes 4 tacos.
1 cup vanilla yogurt
1 teaspoon brown sugar
½ cup strawberries, sliced
Brown Sugar Tortillas (page 140)

Directions:
1. Mix yogurt and brown sugar.
2. Spread about 1½ Tablespoons yogurt and sugar mix on a tortilla. Top with a line of strawberry slices toward one end and roll as tightly as possible without breaking.
3. Serve upside down or with a strawberry on top to hold roll closed!

Tropical Fruit Taco

Makes 3-4 tacos.
¼ cup yogurt (plain or vanilla)
1 mango, peeled and sliced
1 kiwi, peeled, sliced, then halved
¼ cup crushed pineapple, well-drained
Tortillas

Directions:
1. Spread yogurt evenly on a tortilla.
2. Top with fruit.

SPECIALTY

Bean Taquitos
Beef Taquitos
Cheese Taquitos
Hawaiian Pizza Taco
Lamb Meatball Taco
Mac & Cheese Taco
Margherita Pizza Taco
Pepperoni Pizza Taco
St. Patrick's Day Taco
Taco-Stuffed Shells
Thanksgiving Taco

Bean Taquitos

Makes 8 taquitos.
1 can refried beans (16 oz)
Tortillas

DIRECTIONS:
1. Preheat oven to 400°F.
2. Spread about 1½ Tablespoons refried beans evenly across a tortilla so that the entire shell is covered.
3. Starting at the bottom, roll the tortilla up until entire tortilla is rolled in a log. Secure with a toothpick.
4. Place on a baking sheet lined with parchment paper and bake 9-11 minutes, until crispy, but not cracked open.

Beef Taquitos

Makes 5 taquitos.
½ cup ground beef
¼ cup water
1 teaspoon Classic Taco Seasoning (page 170)
1 cup shredded cheddar cheese
Tortillas

DIRECTIONS:
1. Preheat oven to 400°F.
2. Brown ground beef in small sauce pan over medium heat, about 6-8 minutes. Add water and Classic Taco Seasoning, bring to a boil, then reduce to a simmer and cook 4 more minutes.
3. Scatter cheese across a tortilla evenly so that the entire tortilla is loosely covered. Add 1 heaping Tablespoon ground beef in a straight line, about half of an inch thick, as far toward the bottom of the tortilla as possible. Roll the tortilla up over the beef and continue rolling until entire tortilla is rolled in a log. Secure with a toothpick.
4. Place on a baking sheet lined with parchment paper and bake 9-11 minutes, until crispy, but not cracked open.

Cheese Taquitos

Makes 5 taquitos.
2 cups shredded cheddar cheese
Tortillas

Directions:
1. Preheat oven to 400°F.
2. Scatter cheese across a tortilla evenly so that the entire tortilla is densely covered.
3. Starting at the bottom, roll the tortilla up until entire tortilla is rolled in a log. Secure with a toothpick.
4. Place on a baking sheet lined with parchment paper and bake 9-11 minutes, until crispy, but not cracked open.

Hawaiian Pizza Taco

Crisp bacon, a much more taco-friendly ingredient than ham bits, is the star of this taco inspired by one of the best-loved pizzas. If you want to eat a few of these, go a little lighter on the bacon!

Makes 1 taco.
2 Tablespoons tomato sauce
¼ cup shredded cheddar cheese
2 heaping Tablespoons crushed pineapple, drained
1-1½ pieces extra crispy bacon, crumbled
Chopped parsley for topping
Tortilla

Directions:
1. Preheat oven to 400°F.
2. Top a tortilla evenly with all ingredients except parsley and bake 4-5 minutes, until cheese is melted and tortilla is firm but not brittle. Do not overcook or taco will not fold.
3. Top with plenty of parsley.

Lamb Meatball Taco

Makes 8 tacos.

1 pound ground lamb
⅓ cup white onion, very finely chopped
2 Tablespoons cilantro, chopped
2 large garlic cloves, minced
1 teaspoon coriander powder
½ teaspoon cumin powder
½ teaspoon fine ground sea salt
½ teaspoon black pepper
Yogurt Sauce (page 210)
8 pieces lettuce
Paprika for garnish
Chili Lime Tortillas (page 142)

Directions:

1. Preheat oven to 400°F.
2. Mix all ingredients except sauce, lettuce, and tortillas in a medium mixing bowl and roll into small meatballs, about 1 Tablespoon each. Mix should yield about 32 meatballs. Place on a lightly greased baking sheet and cook 16 minutes.
3. Spread 1 teaspoon Yogurt Sauce evenly on a tortilla. Top with 1 piece lettuce and 4 meatballs. Garnish with a pinch of paprika.

Mac & Cheese Taco

Macaroni and cheese shares many of the same ingredients as a taco, so this combo is a no-brainer that is a lot more fun to eat than traditional mac and cheese!

Makes 6-8 tacos.
2 cups shredded cheddar cheese
¼ cup milk
2 cups uncooked elbow macaroni, prepared
Salsa for topping
Cracked black pepper for garnish
Tortillas

DIRECTIONS:
1. In a small nonstick sauce pot, heat cheese and milk until a gooey cheese forms, stirring occasionally, about 2 minutes.
2. Pour cheese on top of cooked elbow macaroni and stir to combine.
3. Top a tortilla with macaroni and cheese, add a fair amount of salsa, and garnish with cracked black pepper.

Margherita Pizza Taco

For a flavorful lunch or easy appetizer in under ten minutes, prepare these tacos that have all the ingredients and flavor of pizza without the grease and heavy feeling in your stomach!

Makes 1 taco.
1 Tablespoon olive oil
2 Tablespoons tomato sauce
1 teaspoon dried basil
1 oz. mozzarella cheese
Fresh basil leaves for topping
Tortilla

DIRECTIONS:

1. Preheat oven to 375°F.
2. Place tortilla on a baking sheet and coat with olive oil.
3. Add tomato sauce evenly and sprinkle dried basil on top.
4. Slice mozzarella into half-inch squares and scatter on sauce. Add fresh basil leaves or reserve for after cooking for brighter color.
5. Bake taco for 5 minutes, until tortilla is firm but not brittle. Do not overcook or taco will not fold.

Pepperoni Pizza Taco

For a deeper flavor than a simple Margherita Pizza Taco that still leaves you feeling light but satisfied, try this taco take on the famous pepperoni pizza. Using pre-sliced pepperoni works best here to achieve the thinness necessary for taco folding without all of the ingredients crumbling to the center of the taco.

Makes 1 taco.
1 Tablespoon olive oil
2 Tablespoons tomato sauce
1 teaspoon oregano
½ teaspoon garlic powder
4 slices pepperoni, quartered
1 pinch red pepper flakes
Tortilla

Directions:
1. Preheat oven to 375°F.
2. Place tortilla on a baking sheet and coat with olive oil.
3. Add tomato sauce evenly and sprinkle dried oregano and garlic powder on top.
4. Scatter pepperoni quarters on sauce and top with red pepper flakes.
5. Bake taco for 5 minutes, until tortilla is firm but not brittle. Do not overcook or taco will not fold.

St. Patrick's Day Taco

Makes 4 tacos.
1 cup boiled cabbage, sliced
1 Tablespoon white vinegar
1 cup prepared corned beef, shredded
⅓ cup Taco Mustard (page 198)
Coarse ground sea salt
Tortillas

Directions:
1. Mix cabbage and vinegar in a medium mixing bowl. Add corned beef and toss.
2. Cover a tortilla with a thin, even layer of Taco Mustard. Top with corned beef and cabbage.
3. Garnish sparingly with sea salt.

Taco-Stuffed Shells

Use a runnier salsa for this (which might mean store-bought), or even go with a spicy tomato sauce.

Makes 16 shells.
1 pound ground beef
1½ Tablespoons Classic Taco Seasoning (page 170)
½ cup water
16 jumbo macaroni shells, cooked
⅓ cup + 1 cup salsa or spicy tomato sauce, separated
⅓ cup shredded cheese (Mexican blend, taco blend, or cheddar)
½ cup sour cream, room temperature

Directions:

1. Preheat oven to 350°F.
2. Brown ground beef in a large pan over medium-high heat, about 8-10 minutes. Drain excess grease, add Classic Taco Seasoning and ½ cup water, and simmer until water is mostly evaporated, about 6-8 minutes.
3. Fill each macaroni shell with a heaping Tablespoon of ground beef and top with a small amount of salsa or spicy tomato sauce (from the ⅓ cup). Place in an oven-safe baking dish and cover (with a lid or aluminum foil). Bake 20 minutes.
4. Add shredded cheese to the top of each shell, and bake 3 more minutes.
5. Meanwhile, bring 1 cup salsa or spicy tomato sauce and sour cream to room temperature and mix together in a small mixing bowl. Use to top shells.

Thanksgiving Taco

If you make this right after Thanksgiving, just use your leftovers as ingredients! Otherwise, follow the directions below for an awesome Thanksgiving treat any time of year!

Makes 8-10 tacos.
1½ pound split turkey breast
2 Tablespoons olive oil
1 scant teaspoon coarse ground sea salt
Cracked black pepper to cover turkey
Paprika to cover turkey
1 can cranberry sauce
2 cups stuffing, prepared
Tortillas

DIRECTIONS:
Preheat oven to 375°F.

1. Cover all sides of turkey breast with olive oil and place in a roasting pan. Sprinkle salt evenly on top of turkey, and cover loosely with cracked black pepper and paprika. Roast until inside is white and juices run clear, about 50-60 minutes. Cool, tented with aluminum foil, 15 minutes. Slice in thin strips.
2. Mix cranberry sauce in a small mixing bowl to create a sauce consistency (instead of a canned mold!). Top a tortilla with a thin, even layer of cranberry sauce.
3. Add a thin layer of stuffing and 2 strips of turkey.

SHELLS

Baked Tortilla (Hard Shell)
Brown Sugar Tortilla
Chili Lime Tortilla
Corn Tortilla
Garlic Ginger Tortilla
Navajo Taco Tortilla
Taco Salad Bowl

Baked Tortilla (Hard Shell)

Making a baked corn tortilla is only one more step than making a soft tortilla! Start with your favorite soft tortilla recipe, then follow the directions below!

Directions:

1. Preheat oven to 375°F.
2. Drape a soft tortilla over one rung of an oven rack positioned in the middle of the oven. Squeeze gently with tongs to encourage sides to fall downward. The tortilla will continue to bend further as it cooks. Cook 8-10 minutes, until tortilla has hardened.
3. Remove from oven with tongs.

Brown Sugar Tortilla

Makes 4 tortillas.
½ cup masa harina
⅓ cup water
Pinch of salt (optional)
1 Tablespoon brown sugar
3 drops pure vanilla extract

Directions:
1. Combine all ingredients in a mixing bowl and blend into a dough.
2. Let sit at least 5 minutes, then form into balls a little smaller than a golf ball.
3. Roll into discs with a rolling pin or use a tortilla press.
4. If dough is too sticky for rolling or pressing, add more masa harina in small increments.
5. If dough is too dry, add more water.
6. Heat tortillas in a hot cast-iron skillet or very hot nonstick pan for one minute on each side until flexibly firm.

Chili Lime Tortilla

Makes 4 tortillas.
½ cup masa harina
⅓ cup water
Pinch of salt (optional)
Zest of 1 lime
2 teaspoons red chili powder

Directions:

1. Combine all ingredients in a mixing bowl and blend into a dough.
2. Let sit at least 5 minutes, then form into balls a little smaller than a golf ball.
3. Roll into discs with a rolling pin or use a tortilla press.
4. If dough is too sticky for rolling or pressing, add more masa harina in small increments.
5. If dough is too dry, add more water.
6. Heat tortillas in a hot cast-iron skillet or very hot nonstick pan for one minute on each side until flexibly firm.

Corn Tortilla

This is the classic soft shell taco tortilla, traditionally made with corn flour (dig in gluten-free taco lovers!). These are much more pliable and flavorful than store-bought corn tortillas and take very little time to make. Make them fresh for each meal, though; they do not keep well. If you make more than you need, cut the leftovers like a pie and bake or fry the triangles for a few minutes to make tortilla chips, which will keep much longer!

Makes 4 tortillas.
½ cup masa harina
⅓ cup water
Pinch of salt (optional)

Directions:
1. Combine all ingredients in a mixing bowl and blend into a dough.
2. Let sit at least 5 minutes, then form into balls a little smaller than a golf ball.
3. Roll into discs with a rolling pin or use a tortilla press.
4. If dough is too sticky for rolling or pressing, add more masa harina in small increments.
5. If dough is too dry, add more water.
6. Heat tortillas in a hot cast-iron skillet or very hot nonstick pan for one minute on each side until flexibly firm.

Garlic Ginger Tortilla

Makes 4 tortillas.
½ cup masa harina
⅓ cup water
Pinch of salt (optional)
2 teaspoons garlic powder
1 teaspoon ginger powder

Directions:
1. Combine all ingredients in a mixing bowl and blend into a dough.
2. Let sit at least 5 minutes, then form into balls a little smaller than a golf ball.
3. Roll into discs with a rolling pin or use a tortilla press.
4. If dough is too sticky for rolling or pressing, add more masa harina in small increments.
5. If dough is too dry, add more water.
6. Heat tortillas in a hot cast-iron skillet or very hot nonstick pan for one minute on each side until flexibly firm.

Navajo Taco Tortilla

Unlike traditional tortillas, this one is made with wheat flour, then fried to golden, puffy deliciousness. You can top it with anything, or even break it apart for use with salsa, but its best use is as the base for the Navajo Taco (page 10).

Makes 4 tortillas.
¾ cup all purpose flour
1 teaspoon baking powder
Dash of salt
¼ cup + 2 Tablespoons warm water
Vegetable oil for frying

DIRECTIONS:

1. Mix flour, baking powder, and salt in a small mixing bowl. Add warm water and work until just combined, but not overworked (do not knead!). Form a ball.
2. With well-floured hands, break the ball into four small balls. Roll into discs with a rolling pin or use a tortilla press. If dough is too sticky for rolling or pressing, add more flour in small increments. If dough is too dry, add more water.
3. Heat an inch of vegetable oil and fry a tortilla until golden brown and crispy, about 45 seconds per side. Tortilla should puff like a pillow.

Taco Salad Bowl

Taco salad bowls are nothing more than large tortillas (burrito size) baked into a bowl shape. There are three easy ways to acquire them:

Purchase ready-made taco salad bowls from well-stocked grocery stores.

Purchase inexpensive taco salad bowl molds from kitchen supply stores and bake large burrito tortillas according to product directions.

Place a large burrito tortilla in an oven-safe bowl and bake at 400°F until crisp and golden, about 10 minutes. If tortilla will not stay down, place a kitchen weight or smaller oven-safe bowl in the middle.

SIDES

30-Minute Chili
Carnitas Rice
Corn Tortilla Crisps
Spicy Tortilla Crisps
Sweet Tortilla Crisps
Sweet Corn Ice Cream
Taco Dip
Taco Dip Cups

30-Minute Chili

Chili is often served as a main course, but this tamed-down recipe makes a perfect side when served in a ramekin or small bowl with the right garnish. Or better yet, put some in a tortilla and make a chili taco!

Makes 6 servings.
1 Tablespoon vegetable oil
½ large yellow onion, diced
6-8 cloves of garlic, crushed and gently chopped
1 carrot, shredded
1 pound ground beef
1 large can diced tomato (28 oz), partially drained (remove about ½ cup of liquid)
2 cans red kidney beans (15.5 oz each)
1 Tablespoon red chili powder
1 teaspoon onion powder
1 teaspoon black pepper
½ teaspoon fine ground sea salt
Shredded cheese (Mexican, taco blend, or cheddar) for topping
Sour cream for topping

Directions:

1. Heat olive oil in a Dutch oven or large pot over medium heat. Add onions and sauté until soft, about 3-4 minutes. Add garlic and carrot and cook for 1 more minute.
2. Add ground beef and cook until brown, about 7-8 minutes.
3. Add tomato, kidney beans, and all seasonings. Stir well, reduce heat to low, and simmer, covered, 15 minutes.
4. Serve hot with a sprinkle of shredded cheese and a dollop of sour cream.

Carnitas Rice

This recipe requires the leftover juices from the preparation of Pork Carnitas to make a satisfying side dish that complements the carnitas without over-filling.

Makes 6-8 servings.
2 cups white rice, uncooked
Chicken broth (amount depends on rice, see below)
1 Tablespoon onion powder
1 teaspoon garlic powder
1 teaspoon fine ground sea salt
Leftover juice from Pork Carnitas (page 68), at least two ladles
Cracked black pepper for garnish
Paprika for garnish

Directions:

1. Prepare any style of white rice according to standard directions, substituting half of the water with chicken broth, and adding onion powder, garlic powder, and sea salt.
2. When rice is finished, transfer to large mixing bowl and add remaining juice from Pork Carnitas. Mix thoroughly.
3. Garnish with cracked black pepper and paprika for color.

Corn Tortilla Crisps

Serve these with your favorite salsa at a party or alongside 30-Minute Chili (page 154) or Taco Dip (page 164)!

Makes 24 crisps.
4 prepared Corn Tortillas (page 144)
Coarse ground sea salt, if desired

Directions:
1. Preheat oven to 375°F.
2. Using a pizza cutter, cut tortilla into 6 equal pieces, like a pie. Add sea salt, if desired.
3. Line a baking pan with parchment paper and spread tortilla slices evenly on top. Bake 18-20 minutes in the center of the oven until crispy throughout. Allow to cool before serving.

Note: For a more traditional chip, skip the baking and fry tortilla triangles in vegetable oil until cripsy and golden, allowing them to cool on a paper-towel-lined plate before serving!

Spicy Tortilla Crisps

Serve these with a refreshing Guacamole (page 184) or Avocado Spread (page 174) as an appetizer, or alongside a mild taco for an added kick to the meal.

Makes 24 crisps.
4 prepared Chili Lime Tortillas (page 142)
Coarse ground sea salt, if desired

Directions:

1. Preheat oven to 375°F.
2. Using a pizza cutter, cut tortilla into 6 equal pieces, like a pie. Add sea salt, if desired.
3. Line a baking pan with parchment paper and spread tortilla slices evenly on top. Bake 18-20 minutes in the center of the oven until crispy throughout. Allow to cool before serving.

Note: For a more traditional chip, skip the baking and fry tortilla triangles in vegetable oil until cripsy and golden, allowing them to cool on a paper-towel-lined plate before serving!

Sweet Tortilla Crisps

Serve these with Sweet Corn Ice Cream (page 162) for dessert, or with any spicy taco for a bit of relief.

Makes 24 crisps.
4 prepared Brown Sugar Tortillas (page 140)
Brown sugar, if desired

Directions:
1. Preheat oven to 375°F.
2. Using a pizza cutter, cut tortilla into 6 equal pieces, like a pie. Top with a sprinkling of additional brown sugar, if desired.
3. Line a baking pan with parchment paper and spread tortilla slices evenly on top. Bake 18-20 minutes in the center of the oven until crispy throughout. Allow to cool before serving.

Note: For a more traditional chip, skip the baking and fry tortilla triangles in vegetable oil until cripsy and golden, allowing them to cool on a paper-towel-lined plate before serving!

Sweet Corn Ice Cream

Serve as an exciting side to a spicy taco for sweet relief, or have some for dessert! Use regular corn (1 large fresh corn cob should do, and canned whole kernels, drained, will also work); there is plenty of sweetness in the rest of the ingredients!

Makes 4-6 servings.
2 Tablespoons butter
2 cups corn kernels
¼ cup sugar
½ teaspoon salt
1 pinch black pepper
2 cups heavy cream
1 cup half and half
2 Tablespoons honey
¼ teaspoon vanilla

Directions:

1. Melt butter in a medium saucepan over medium heat. Add corn, sugar, salt, and pepper, and cook 10 minutes until corn begins to turn to turn gold (lightly caramelized).
2. Mix heavy cream, half and half, honey, and vanilla in a mixing bowl and add to corn. Bring to a boil and turn off heat.
3. When mixture has cooled, at least ten minutes, blend in a food processor until smooth. Pass through a fine sieve. Cover and refrigerate at least 2½ hours, then mix in an ice cream maker according to the product's instructions.
4. Cover and refrigerate at least 4 hours, preferably overnight, before serving.

Taco Dip

This 7-layer (8 if you add black olives!) is a quick and easy dish that presents beautifully as an appetizer or party dish. The key to a great taco dip is to be sparing with the sour cream, which has a surprising potential to drown the great flavor of the other ingredients if used too heavily.

Serves 8-10 guests as an appetizer, more at a party buffet.
1 can refried beans (16 oz)
3 Tablespoons Classic Taco Seasoning (page 170)
1 container sour cream (8 oz)
2 cups Salsa (page 192 or 194)
1 cup iceberg lettuce, shredded
2 medium tomatoes, diced
1 bunch green onions, chopped
2 cups of shredded cheese (taco blend or Mexican blend)
1 small can sliced black olives (2 oz), optional
Corn Tortilla Crisps (page 158) for scooping (fried works better than baked, here)

DIRECTIONS:

1. Heat beans and Classic Taco Seasoning, mixed well, in a large skillet over medium heat until warm throughout, about 3-4 minutes. Spread seasoned beans in an even layer in a glass baking dish.
2. Add a thin layer of sour cream over the beans and top with an even layer of salsa.
3. Add a thin layer of lettuce and top with tomato, green onions, and shredded cheese.
4. Add black olives if desired and serve with tortilla chips.
5. Refrigerate leftovers.

Taco Dip Cups

Want personal taco dip servings in individual bowls to pair with a meal or present at a party? Try this super fast recipe to get a great response from your guests for little effort.

Makes 4 generous taco cups.
1 can refried beans (16 oz)
1 cup sour cream
1 Tablespoon Classic Taco Seasoning (page 170) + 1 teaspoon for garnish
1 medium tomato, diced
1 cup shredded cheese (taco blend or Mexican blend)
Green onions for garnish
Black olives for garnish (optional)
Corn Tortilla Crisps (page 158) for serving (fried works better than baked, here)

DIRECTIONS:

1. Spread refried beans into even layers in single-serving ramekins (5 oz).
2. Mix sour cream and Classic Taco Seasoning in small mixing bowl, then layer over beans.
3. Top with diced tomato, shredded cheese, green onions, and black olives if desired.
4. Serve with a chip spiked in the dip, and plenty more chips for dipping.

SEASONINGS & SAUCES

Classic Taco Seasoning
Spicy Grill Rub
Avocado Spread
Baja Taco Sauce
Black Bean & Corn Salsa
Chickpea & White Bean Hummus
Chipotle Salsa
Guacamole
Mango Salsa
Pesto
Pico de Gallo
Salsa, Hot
Salsa, Mild
Taco Aioli
Taco Mayonnaise
Taco Mustard
Taco Russian Dressing
Taco Salad Dressing
Taco Sauce
Tahini
Tzatziki
Yogurt Sauce

Classic Taco Seasoning

Makes slightly under ½ cup.

2 Tablespoons chili powder
1½ Tablespoons ground cumin
2 teaspoons paprika
2 teaspoons garlic powder
1½ teaspoons black pepper
1½ teaspoons onion powder
1½ teaspoons coarse ground sea salt
¾ teaspoon crushed red pepper flakes
¾ teaspoon dried oregano

DIRECTIONS:

1. Mix all ingredients in a small mixing bowl.
2. Store in an airtight container.

Spicy Grill Rub

Makes slightly under ¼ cup.

2 Tablespoons coarse ground pepper
1 Tablespoon onion powder
½ Tablespoon red chili powder
½ Tablespoon garlic powder
½ Tablespoon fine ground sea salt
½ Tablespoon dried oregano

Directions:

1. Mix all ingredients in a small mixing bowl.
2. Store in an airtight container.

Avocado Spread

Simpler than guacamole, avocado spread adds a touch of flavor without overpowering the taco's main ingredients.

Makes about ½ cup.
½ avocado
2 Tablespoons sour cream

Directions:

1. Scoop the avocado from its shell and add contents to a small mixing bowl. Add sour cream and mix all ingredients until mostly smooth.
2. Refrigerate leftovers.

Baja Taco Sauce

Use this on fish tacos of all kinds, or serve it with homemade fish sticks for a gourmet treat!

Makes ½ cup.
½ cup sour cream
1 teaspoon paprika
2 Tablespoons chopped cilantro
Juice of ½ small lime
½ teaspoon fine ground sea salt

DIRECTIONS:
1. Mix all ingredients in small mixing bowl.
2. Refrigerate leftovers.

Black Bean & Corn Salsa

Makes 3 cups.

Kernels of 1 ear of corn
1 can black beans (14.5 oz), drained
1 Tablespoon olive oil
Juice of ½ lime
1 Tablespoon paprika
½ Tablespoon cumin
1 teaspoon garlic powder

Directions:

1. Mix all ingredients in a medium mixing bowl.
2. Refrigerate at least 30 minutes.
3. Refrigerate leftovers.

Chickpea & White Bean Hummus

Makes about 3 cups.

2 cans garbanzo beans (15.5 oz each), drained, reserving 4 cups of juice
1 cup white beans (about half a can)
1½ Tablespoons olive oil
1 Tablespoon lemon juice
½ teaspoon garlic powder
½ teaspoon red chili powder
½ teaspoon fine ground kosher sea salt

DIRECTIONS:

1. Blend all ingredients in a food processor until smooth.
2. Refrigerate leftovers.

Chipotle Salsa

Makes 2 cups.

1 can peeled whole tomatoes, with juice
2 large chipotle peppers
1 teaspoon cumin
1 scant teaspoon fine ground sea salt
1 Tablespoon olive oil
1 large plum tomato, diced
4 large garlic cloves, minced
¼ red onion, finely diced

Directions:

1. Add canned tomatoes, chipotle peppers, cumin, salt, and olive oil to a food processor, and blend until smooth.
2. Combine in a medium mixing bowl with remaining ingredients.
3. Refrigerate at least 30 minutes.
4. Refrigerate leftovers.

Guacamole

Light, refreshing, and salty, everyone loves chilled guacamole served with chips, on top of a taco, or even as a sandwich spread. Try it on top of 30-Minute Chili (page 154) instead of sour cream!

Makes 1½ cups.
2 avocados
¼ cup finely diced red onion
Juice of ½ lime
1 heaping teaspoon coarse ground sea salt
¼ cup tomato, chopped just before serving

DIRECTIONS:
1. Halve and seed the avocados, then scoop the flesh into a medium mixing bowl. Gently mash the avocado with a fork to break down, but leave some chunkiness.
2. Add red onion, lime, and salt, and mix gently. Refrigerate at least 30 minutes.
3. Before serving, chop and add tomato, and mix gently one last time.

Mango Salsa

For a sweet and spicy boost, add a Tablespoon or two of this to a pork or fish taco. This is also a perfect salsa for tortilla chips!

Makes about 1½ cups.
1 mango, diced fine
¼ cup finely diced tomato
¼ teaspoon chili powder
1 scallion, chopped
Juice of ½ small lime
2 teaspoons lemon juice
Dash of salt

DIRECTIONS:
1. Combine all ingredients in a mixing bowl and chill at least 15 minutes.
2. Refrigerate leftovers.

Pesto

Pesto for a taco? Absolutely! You can use it as a spread for any vegetable taco you create, but be sure to try it with the Zucchini Pesto Taco (page 98).

Makes about 1 cup.
2 cups fresh basil
⅓ cup walnuts (pine nuts are traditional, and also an option), crushed
4 cloves garlic, minced
½ teaspoon fine ground sea salt
½-1 cup olive oil

DIRECTIONS:
1. Add basil, walnuts, garlic, and salt to a food processor, and pulse 5 times.
2. Turn the food processor on and slowly add olive oil in a steady stream to create a sauce. Add more or less oil to reach your desired consistency. A less wet sauce is better for a taco.

Note: Feel free to add ½ cup of grated Parmesan or Romano cheese before adding the oil for richer flavor!

Pico de Gallo

A simple, beautiful, refreshing salsa great on a simple chicken taco and *perfect* for salty chips. The ingredients are traditionally chopped very fine, but larger chunks can provide better bursts of flavor!

Makes about 2 cups.
2 plum tomatoes, chopped fine
1 medium white onion, chopped fine (about 1 cup)
1 jalapeno, or other hot pepper, chopped fine
Juice of ½ lime

DIRECTIONS:
1. Mix all ingredients in a medium mixing bowl.
2. Refrigerate leftovers.

Salsa, Hot

A hotter salsa works better when there are more juices to spread the flavor, so give this a good mash before refrigerating.

Makes about 1½ cups.
2 plum tomatoes, chopped
¼ cup red onion, diced
1 scallion, chopped
1 Tablespoon olive oil
Juice of ½ lime
1 jalapeno pepper (or other small hot pepper) with seeds, chopped
1 scant teaspoon garlic powder
½ teaspoon cumin powder
½ teaspoon red chili powder
½ teaspoon coarse ground sea salt
A few drops of hot sauce, if high heat is desired

DIRECTIONS:

1. Combine ingredients in a medium mixing bowl. Mash several times with a meat tenderizer, a pestle, or any other solid gadget to release a fair amount of juices.
2. Refrigerate at least 15 minutes.
3. Refrigerate leftovers.

Salsa, Mild

A nice mild salsa should be mostly chunky, so just whip together the following ingredients, stir a few times, and refrigerate!

Makes about 2 cups.
2 plum tomatoes, chopped
¼ cup red onion, diced
1 scallion, chopped
1 Tablespoon olive oil
Juice of ½ lime
1 scant teaspoon garlic powder
½ teaspoon cumin powder
½ teaspoon paprika
½ teaspoon coarse ground sea salt

Directions:
1. Combine ingredients in a medium mixing bowl. Stir gently to mix.
2. Refrigerate at least 15 minutes.
3. Refrigerate leftovers.

Taco Aioli

Makes 1 cup.

1 cup mayonnaise
1 Tablespoon olive oil
1 teaspoon lemon juice
1 teaspoon garlic powder
1 teaspoon dried oregano
½ teaspoon paprika
½ teaspoon black pepper
½ teaspoon fine ground sea salt

DIRECTIONS:

1. Mix all ingredients in a small mixing bowl.
2. Refrigerate leftovers.

Taco Mayonnaise

Makes ¼ cup.
¼ cup mayonnaise
1 teaspoon cumin
1 teaspoon paprika

DIRECTIONS:
1. Mix all ingredients in a small blender.
2. Store leftovers in the refrigerator.

Taco Mustard

Makes about 1 cup.

¾ cup sour cream
½ cup yellow mustard
1 Tablespoon lemon juice
1 teaspoon cumin
1 teaspoon paprika
½ teaspoon black pepper
½ teaspoon fine ground sea salt

Directions:

1. Blend all ingredients in a mixing bowl.
2. Refrigerate leftovers.

Taco Russian Dressing

Makes about ¾ cup.
⅓ cup mayonnaise
3 Tablespoons ketchup
3 Tablespoons relish
1 scant teaspoon Classic Taco Seasoning (page 170)

Directions:
1. Combine all ingredients in a small mixing bowl and mix thoroughly.
2. Refrigerate leftovers.

Taco Salad Dressing

This is a delicious dressing with the perfect consistency for a taco salad. Best of all, it only uses two ingredients, both of which go on many tacos!

Makes 2 cups.
½ cup sour cream
1½ cups Mild Salsa (page 194)

DIRECTIONS:
1. Mix sour cream and Mild Salsa thoroughly in a mixing bowl.
2. Refrigerate leftovers.

Taco Sauce

None of the recipes in this book call for taco sauce, but you may find that you want it anyway, so here are simple options for homemade taco sauce, both mild and hot!

Mild Taco Sauce

Makes just over 10 ounces.

1 jar of thin tomato sauce (8 ounces)
¼ cup water
1 Tablespoon white vinegar
1 teaspoon onion powder
1 teaspoon garlic powder
½ teaspoon cumin
¼ teaspoon fine ground sea salt
¼ teaspoon paprika
¼ teaspoon sugar

Hot Taco Sauce

Follow directions for Mild Taco Sauce (left), adding the following ingredients:

1 teaspoon red chili powder
½ teaspoon hot sauce
¼ teaspoon black pepper

Directions:

1. Add all ingredients in a food processor until smooth.
2. Bring to a boil in a medium sauce pan, reduce heat to low, and simmer 10 minutes.
3. Refrigerate at least 30 minutes before using.
4. Refrigerate leftovers.

Tahini

Tahini is most often used as an ingredient in hummus, but it is a great addition to any recipe involving vegetables (especially raw), falafel, beans, or rices.

Makes about 1 cup.
1½ cups sesame seeds
¼ cup olive oil

DIRECTIONS:
1. Preheat oven to 375°F.
2. Spread sesame seeds on a baking sheet and bake until fragrant but not brown, about 8 minutes, shaking often.
3. Combine sesame seeds and oil in a food processor and blend until smooth.
4. Refrigerate leftovers.

Tzatziki

Makes ½ cup.
½ cup yogurt
½ cucumber, peeled, seeded, and finely diced
1 Tablespoon olive oil
1 scant teaspoon garlic powder

Directions:
1. Mix all ingredients in a small mixing bowl.
2. Refrigerate leftovers.

Yogurt Sauce

Makes 1 cup.
1 cup greek yogurt
1 scant Tablespoon cumin powder
1 teaspoon coriander powder
1 teaspoon lemon juice
1 heaping Tablespoon chopped cilantro

Directions:
1. Mix all ingredients in a medium mixing bowl.
2. Refrigerate leftovers.

LEFTOVER TACO

The Leftover Taco deserves its own section because it illustrates the very essence of what a taco truly is—just a meal in a tortilla—and symbolizes the limitless potential of taco wizardry. In the same way that you can turn most leftovers into a casserole, an omelet, or a stirfry, just about any small serving can be piled onto a tortilla and made into a taco. Just remember to keep the liquid content low and the ingredients in small pieces.

Makes whatever you have left.
Leftovers
Tortillas

Directions:
1. Chop leftovers to taco-appropriate proportions, and drain any liquids.
2. Top a tortilla with leftovers.

TACO PARTY

Taco Party

If you have a bunch of people coming over (5, 20, or even more!), a taco party is an easy and fun way to ensure that everyone gets plenty to eat and has plenty of options to respect allergies, sensitivities, and preferences! And the presentation options are plentiful, too.

The primary considerations here are a large enough table or counter space, plenty of bowls for ingredients (think salad bar), and plenty of tortillas! Plan on at least 4 tortillas for each guest (and you) if you are using traditional size tortillas, and 2-3 if you are using large, burrito size tortillas.

Vegetarian taco ingredients are easiest for a larger party, as the ingredients are likely to be just as tasty at room temperature, or even cold, and can be prepared in large quantities in advance, but try not to shy away from delicious meats that are sure to please most crowds. You can prepare large amounts of slow roasted pork, chicken, and beef, and keep them covered in the oven (turned off, of course!) until your spread requires refills.

Classic American Taco ingredients will be most recognizable to guests, but I urge you to branch out and prepare stuffings of a more unusual nature if you really want to impress. Your guests make ground beef tacos at home, but have they ever made a Zucchini Pesto Taco or a Sausage & Peppers Taco? Probably not. Stuffings like these are easy to prepare in bulk and will make your taco party one to remember.

Presentation is simple: many ingredients in many bowls, scattered across a whole table (or counter). If this party is on the nicer side, put boxes and containers of varying heights around the table before covering with a cloth to create tiers for your ingredients, and scatter edible garnishes like limes and herbs for a non-cheesy taco theme.

Word of caution: Though tacos may be considered humble finger foods of an often casual nature, I recommend using sturdy plates (not paper plates) for a taco party of any variety. Tacos are sometimes messy foods and ingredients and sauces are sure to drop from tortillas, so make sure your guests have plates that are not also going to drop these morsels.

CONVERSIONS

METRIC AND IMPERIAL CONVERSIONS

(These conversions are rounded for convenience)

Ingredient	Cups/Tablespoons/ Teaspoons	Ounces	Grams/Milliliters
Butter	1 cup=16 tablespoons= 2 sticks	8 ounces	230 grams
Cream cheese	1 tablespoon	0.5 ounce	14.5 grams
Cheese, shredded	1 cup	4 ounces	110 grams
Cornstarch	1 tablespoon	0.3 ounce	8 grams
Flour, all-purpose	1 cup/1 tablespoon	4.5 ounces/0.3 ounce	125 grams/8 grams
Flour, whole wheat	1 cup	4 ounces	120 grams
Fruit, dried	1 cup	4 ounces	120 grams
Fruits or veggies, chopped	1 cup	5 to 7 ounces	145 to 200 grams
Fruits or veggies, puréed	1 cup	8.5 ounces	245 grams
Honey, maple syrup, or corn syrup	1 tablespoon	.75 ounce	20 grams
Liquids: cream, milk, water, or juice	1 cup	8 fluid ounces	240 milliliters
Oats	1 cup	5.5 ounces	150 grams
Salt	1 teaspoon	0.2 ounces	6 grams
Spices: cinnamon, cloves, ginger, or nutmeg (ground)	1 teaspoon	0.2 ounce	5 milliliters
Sugar, brown, firmly packed	1 cup	7 ounces	200 grams
Sugar, white	1 cup/1 tablespoon	7 ounces/0.5 ounce	200 grams/12.5 grams
Vanilla extract	1 teaspoon	0.2 ounce	4 grams

OVEN TEMPERATURES

Fahrenheit	Celcius	Gas Mark
225°	110°	¼
250°	120°	½
275°	140°	1
300°	150°	2
325°	160°	3
350°	180°	4
375°	190°	5
400°	200°	6
425°	220°	7
450°	230°	8

RECIPE INDEX

Recipe Index

RECIPE REFERENCES

Recipe References

Ian's Dry Rub	44 (Southwestern Smoked Chicken Taco)
Ian's Tomatillo Jam	44 (Southwestern Smoked Chicken Taco)
Mango Salsa	50 (Baja Fish Taco)
Mild Salsa	6 (Classic American Taco)
	32 (Chili Lime Chicken Taco)
	106 (Mexican Scrambled Egg Taco)
	108 (Southwestern Omelet Taco)
	164 (Taco Dip)
	202 (Taco Salad Dressing)
Navajo Taco	148 (Navajo Taco Tortilla)
Navajo Taco Shell	10 (Navajo Taco)
Pesto	98(Zucchini Pesto Taco)
Pork Carnitas	156 (Carnitas Rice)
Spicy Grill Rub	38 (Grilled Chicken Taco)
Sweet Corn Ice Cream	161 (Sweet Tortilla Crisps)
Taco Aioli	62 (BLT Taco)
	84 (Roasted Vegetable Taco)
Taco Dip	158 (Corn Tortilla Crisps)
Taco Mayonnaise	96 (Waldorf Taco)
Taco Mustard	56 (Tuna Salad Taco)
	66 (New Year's Taco)
	130 (St. Patrick's Day Taco)
Taco Russian Dressing	14 (Reuben Taco)
Taco Salad Bowl	16 (Santa Fe Taco Salad)
	18 (Traditional Taco Salad)
Taco Salad Dressing	18 (Traditional Taco Salad)
Taco Sauce	6 (Classic American Taco)
	38 (Grilled Chicken Taco)
Tahini	78 (Falafel Tahini Taco)
Tzatziki	8 (Greek Taco)
Yogurt Sauce	122 (Lamb Meatball Taco)
Zucchini Pesto Taco	188 (Pesto)

ACKNOWLEDGMENTS